THE
100
GREATEST
LEADERSHIP PRINCIPLES
OF ALL TIME

Also edited by Leslie Pockell and Adrienne Avila

The 100 Best Poems of All Time
The 100 Best Love Poems of All Time
The 13 Best Horror Stories of All Time
Everything I've Learned
The 101 Greatest Business Principles of All Time
The 100 Greatest Sales Tips of All Time
Only the Best/Solo lo Mejor

THE
100
GREATEST
LEADERSHIP PRINCIPLES
OF ALL TIME

EDITED BY
LESLIE POCKELL
WITH
ADRIENNE AVILA

WARNER
BUSINESS
BOOKS™

NEW YORK   BOSTON

Warner Business Books
Hachette Book Group USA
237 Park Avenue
New York, NY 10169
Visit our Web site at www.HachetteBookGroupUSA.com.

Warner Business Books is an imprint of Warner Books
Warner Business Books is a trademark of Time Warner Inc. or an affiliated
company. Used under license by Hachette Book Group USA, which is not
affiliated with Time Warner Inc.

Printed in the United States of America

First Edition: August 2007

10 9 8 7 6 5 4 3 2 1

ISBN-10: 0-446-57991-2
ISBN-13: 978-0-446-57991-9
LCCN: 2006934325

INTRODUCTION

Leadership is a matter of intelligence, trustworthiness, humaneness, courage, and discipline . . . Reliance on intelligence alone results in rebelliousness. Exercise of humaneness alone results in weakness. Fixation on trust results in folly. Dependence on the strength of courage results in violence. Excessive discipline and sternness in command result in cruelty. When one has all five virtues together, each appropriate to its function, then one can be a leader.

— Sun Tzu

Sun Tzu's *Art of War* originally was intended to be read as a work of military strategy and philosophy. Yet even today, more than 2,000 years later, Sun Tzu's description of the traits that characterize a successful leader is valid in any arena—war, politics, business, and any endeavor that requires the ability to inspire and mobilize the efforts of a group in the service of a common goal.

Taking Sun Tzu's categories as a point of departure, this book is divided into five sections, each one containing twenty quotations that offer different perspectives on the requirements of leadership. The attentive reader will note that some of the principles seem to comment on others in different sections; for example, in the section on Trustworthiness, Douglas McArthur is quoted as saying "Never give an order that can't be obeyed"; while in the section on Discipline, these words of Sophocles appear: "What you cannot enforce, do not command." Almost the same sentiment, but not quite—Sophocles focuses on the leader, and McArthur on the led. It's in the conjunction of similar and even sometimes apparently conflicting principles that a three-dimensional image of the leader is intended to emerge.

What kind of person is the theoretical ideal leader?

The ideal leader has the intelligence to understand the subtleties and complexity of the leadership role: It is not sufficient to bear the title and hold the authority of a leader to function as one. The very concept of leadership is subjective, which is why so many different varieties and degrees of leadership are evident in society and in business. The perfect leader understands what it means to lead, and to be led.

The ideal leader is aware of the mutual responsibility of the leader and the led: Each relies on and supports the other. A leader without a sense of humanity is only a leader by virtue of superior power, while a great leader inspires more by force of character and principle than by fear and intimidation.

The ideal leader is also someone who can be trusted. England's King Charles II was notoriously described as one "whose word no man relies on." For all his cleverness, he did not go down in history as a great leader; he never trusted anyone, and no one trusted him. The essence of trust and trustworthiness is the necessity of interdependence. If a leader loses the confidence of those who follow, they will cease to follow; if a leader fails to trust the skills of those who follow, the result will be disaster. No one can lead alone; the concept is absurd.

A successful leader is courageous, and not simply in the physical sense. Many decisions must be made in solitude, even when the leader has numerous counselors. The perfect leader is one who willingly takes on the responsibility for advancing or retreating, and accepts the consequences. If the leader is not seen to have the courage required to act on behalf of all, the leader will lose the confidence of the group, and ultimately the position of leadership itself.

Finally, the perfect leader must impose discipline, in the classic sense of teaching followers the correct path. Discipline is not simply exercising control and punishing those who fail to obey instructions. Discipline is guidance, structure, training; without it, no one can lead effectively.

Sun Tzu pointed out that each of the qualities he mentions as essential for leadership can lead to excess and abuse. It is only by balancing the proportions of these qualities that the leader can attain maximum effectiveness. We hope that in reading and contemplating the principles in this book, you will find your own personal path to leadership.

We would like to thank our publisher, Jamie Raab, and our editor, Rick Wolff, for their support of this project.

Leslie Pockell
Adrienne Avila

CONTENTS

THE
100
GREATEST
LEADERSHIP PRINCIPLES
OF ALL TIME

PART 1

Intelligence

Many people have ideas on how others should change; few people have ideas on how they should change.

Leo Tolstoy

It's amazing how many cares disappear
when you decide not to be something,
but to be someone.

🍂

Coco Chanel

The only real training for
leadership is leadership.

Anthony Jay

The ultimate leader is one who is willing to develop people to the point that they surpass him or her in knowledge and ability.

Fred A. Manske

A genuine leader is not a searcher for consensus but a molder of consensus.

Martin Luther King, Jr.

Do not go where the path may lead.
Go instead where there is no path
and leave a trail.

Ralph Waldo Emerson

Forethought and prudence are the
proper qualities of a leader.

Tacitus

A true leader always keeps an element of surprise up his sleeve, which others cannot grasp but which keeps his public excited and breathless.

Charles deGaulle

Those who know how to win are more numerous than those who know how to make proper use of their victories.

Polybius

If a man does not know to what port he is steering, no wind is favorable to him.

Seneca

I used to think that running an organization was equivalent to conducting a symphony orchestra. But I don't think that's quite it; it's more like jazz. There is more improvisation.

Warren Bennis

The first method for estimating the
intelligence of a ruler is to look at
the men he has around him.

Niccolo Machiavelli

The chief executive who knows his strengths and weaknesses as a leader is likely to be far more effective than the one who remains blind to them. He also is on the road to humility— that priceless attitude of openness to life that can help a manager absorb mistakes, failures, or personal shortcomings.

John Adair

Management is efficiency in climbing
the ladder of success; leadership
determines whether the ladder is
leaning against the right wall.

Stephen R. Covey

One of the tests of leadership is to
recognize a problem before
it becomes an emergency.

Arnold Glasow

There's nothing more demoralizing than a leader who can't clearly articulate why we're doing what we're doing.

James Kouzes and Barry Posner

There are no mistakes so great as
that of being always right.

Samuel Butler

You can use all the quantitative data you can get, but you still have to distrust it and use your own intelligence and judgment.

Alvin Toffler

A leader is one who sees more than others see,
who sees farther than others see, and
who sees before others see.

Leroy Eimes

Great spirits have always found violent opposition from mediocrities. The latter cannot understand it when a man does not thoughtlessly submit to hereditary prejudices but honestly and courageously uses his intelligence.

Albert Einstein

PART 2

Trustworthiness

We must become the change
we want to see.

Mahatma Gandhi

A good leader can't get too far
ahead of his followers.

Franklin D. Roosevelt

Never give an order that can't be obeyed.

Douglas MacArthur

I cannot trust a man to control others
who cannot control himself.

Robert E. Lee

No man is wise enough by himself.

Plautus

No man will make a great leader who
wants to do it all himself,
or to get all the credit for doing it.

Andrew Carnegie

You don't have to hold a position
in order to be a leader.

Anthony D'Angelo

I have yet to find the man, however exalted his station, who did not do better work and put forth greater effort under a spirit of approval than under a spirit of criticism.

Charles Schwab

Never hire or promote in your own image. It is foolish to replicate your strength and idiotic to replicate your weakness. It is essential to employ, trust, and reward those whose perspective, ability, and judgment are radically different from yours. It is also rare, for it requires uncommon humility, tolerance, and wisdom.

Dee W. Hock

Help others get ahead. You will always stand taller with someone else on your shoulders.

Bob Moawad

The leaders who work most effectively, it seems to me, never say "I." And that's not because they have trained themselves not to say "I." They don't think "I." They think "we"; they think "team." They understand their job to be to make the team function. They accept responsibility and don't sidestep it, but "we" gets the credit . . . This is what creates trust, what enables you to get the task done.

Peter F. Drucker

It is important that an aim never be defined in terms of activity or methods. It must always relate directly to how life is better for everyone . . . The aim of the system must be clear to everyone in the system. The aim must include plans for the future. The aim is a value judgment.

W. Edwards Deming

Treat people as if they were what they ought
to be and you help them to become what
they are capable of being.

Johann Wolfgang von Goethe

One measure of leadership is the caliber of people who choose to follow you.

❧

Dennis A. Peer

A true leader has to have a genuine open-door policy so that his people are not afraid to approach him for any reason.

Harold Geneen

Leadership is getting people to work for you
when they are not obligated.

Fred Smith

A leader leads by example,

whether he intends to or not.

Anonymous

Delegating work works, provided
the one delegating works too.

Robert Half

Leaders are dealers in hope.

Napoleon

The first responsibility of a leader is to define
reality. The last is to say "thank you."
In between, the leader is a servant.

Max DePree

PART 3

Humaneness

The man whose authority is recent
is always stern.

Aeschylus

Be kind, for everyone you meet is
fighting a hard battle.

Plato

To lead people, walk beside them . . .

As for the best leaders, the people do not
  notice their existence.

The next best, the people honor and praise.

The next, the people fear;
  and the next, the people hate . . .

When the best leader's work is done the
  people say,

"We did it ourselves!"

Lao-tse

You do not lead by hitting people over the head—that's assault, not leadership.

Dwight D. Eisenhower

Leadership is a combination of strategy and
character. If you must be without one,
be without the strategy.

H. Norman Schwarzkopf

Leadership is solving problems. The day soldiers stop bringing you their problems is the day you have stopped leading them. They have either lost confidence that you can help or concluded you do not care. Either case is a failure of leadership.

Karl Popper

He makes a great mistake, who supposes that authority is firmer or better established when it is founded by force than that which is welded by affection.

Terence

Lead and inspire people. Don't try to manage and manipulate people. Inventories can be managed but people must be led.

Ross Perot

There go my people. I must find out where they are going so I can lead them.

Alexandre Auguste Ledru-Rollin

People ask the difference between a leader and a boss . . . The leader leads, and the boss drives.

Theodore Roosevelt

The boss drives his men; the leader coaches them. The boss depends upon authority; the leader on good will. The boss inspires fear; the leader inspires enthusiasm. The boss says "I"; the leader "we." The boss fixes the blame for the breakdown; the leader fixes the breakdown. The boss says "go"; the leader says "let's go!"

Gordon Selfridge

The highest proof of virtue is to possess
boundless power without abusing it.

Thomas Babington Macaulay

Do you wish to rise? Begin by descending.
You plan a tower that will pierce the clouds?
Lay first the foundation of humility.

St. Augustine

In order to make a fire burn, you fan the live coals. In order to keep your organization fired up, it's imperative that you find and motivate the leaders or potential leaders in your organization regardless of how far down the line they might be.

Dexter Yager

Knowledge alone is not enough to get desired results. You must have the more elusive ability to teach and to motivate. This defines a leader; if you can't teach and you can't motivate, you can't lead.

John Wooden

Leaders focus on the soft stuff. People. Values. Character. Commitment. A cause. All of the stuff that was supposed to be too goo-goo to count in business. Yet it's the stuff that real leaders take care of first. And forever. That's why leadership is an art, not a science.

Tom Peters

Nobody rises to low expectations.

Calvin Lloyd

The leader has to be practical and a realist,
yet must talk the language of the
visionary and the idealist.

Eric Hoffer

Leaders must be close enough to
relate to others, but far enough ahead
to motivate them.

John Maxwell

If I have seen further, it is by standing on the shoulders of giants.

Isaac Newton

PART 4

Courage

Abraham Lincoln did not go to Gettysburg having commissioned a poll to find out what would sell in Gettysburg. There were no people with percentages for him, cautioning him about this group or that group or what they found in exit polls a year earlier. When will we have the courage of Lincoln?

Robert Coles

You've got to jump off cliffs all the time and build your wings on the way down.

Ray Bradbury

The trouble is, if you don't risk anything,

you risk even more.

Erica Jong

In matters of style, swim with the current;
in matters of principle, stand like a rock.

Thomas Jefferson

Not the cry, but the flight of the wild duck,
leads the flock to fly and follow.

Chinese proverb

Leadership is action, not position.

Donald H. McGannon

Self-assurance is two-thirds of success.

Gaelic proverb

A brave captain is as a root, out of which,

as branches, the courage of his

soldiers doth spring.

Sir Philip Sidney

If the leader is filled with high ambition and
if he pursues his aims with audacity and
strength of will, he will reach them
in spite of all obstacles.

Karl von Clausewitz

The charismatic leader gains and
maintains authority solely by
proving his strength in life.

Max Weber

Anyone can hold the helm

when the sea is calm.

Publilius Syrus

It's hard to lead a cavalry charge if you think you look funny on a horse.

Adlai Stevenson

The only way around is through.

Robert Frost

An army of sheep led by a lion would defeat an army of lions led by a sheep.

Arab proverb

A leader must have the courage to
act against an expert's advice.

James Callaghan

"Safety first" has been the motto of the human race for half a million years; but it has never been the motto of leaders. A leader must face danger. He must take the risk and the blame, and the brunt of the storm.

Herbert N. Casson

If it's a good idea, go ahead and do it.
It is much easier to apologize than
it is to get permission.

Grace Hopper

Don't be afraid to take a big step when one is indicated. You can't cross a chasm in two small steps.

❧

David Lloyd George

Most companies don't die because they are wrong; most die because they don't commit themselves . . . You have to have a strong leader setting a direction. And it doesn't even have to be the best direction—just a strong, clear one.

Andy Grove

Leaders are visionaries with a poorly developed sense of fear and no concept of the odds against them.

Dr. Robert Jarvik

PART 5

Discipline

Mountaintops inspire leaders
but valleys mature them.

⌖

Winston Churchill

All men can stand adversity, but if you want to test a man's character, give him power.

Abraham Lincoln

It is not fair to ask of others what you are unwilling to do yourself.

Anna Eleanor Roosevelt

Example is leadership.

Albert Schweitzer

What you cannot enforce, do not command.

Sophocles

Half of the harm that is done in this world is due to people who want to feel important . . . They do not mean to do harm . . . They are absorbed in the endless struggle to think well of themselves.

T.S. Eliot

Be willing to make decisions. That's the most important quality in a good leader. Don't fall victim to what I call the "ready-aim-aim-aim syndrome." You must be willing to fire.

George S. Patton

The speed of the leader determines
the rate of the pack.

D. Wayne Lukas

The spirited horse, which will try to
win the race of its own accord,
will run even faster if encouraged.

Ovid

A community is like a ship: Everyone ought
to be prepared to take the helm.

Henrik Ibsen

For if the trumpet give an uncertain sound,
who shall prepare himself to the battle?

St. Paul

Have patience. All things are difficult

before they become easy.

❦

Saadi Shirazi

It is always easier to dismiss a man than it is to train him. No great leader ever built a reputation on firing people. Many have built a reputation on developing them.

Anonymous

I am a man of fixed and unbending principles,
the first of which is to be flexible at all times.

Everett Dirksen

To be a leader of men, one must turn
one's back on men.

Havelock Ellis

Leadership is a matter of having people look at you and gain confidence, seeing how you react. If you're in control, they're in control.

Tom Landry

In simplest terms, a leader is one who knows where he wants to go, and gets up, and goes.

John Erskine

Leadership consists not in degrees of technique but in traits of character; it requires moral rather than athletic or intellectual effort, and it imposes on both leader and follower alike the burdens of self-restraint.

Lewis H. Lapham

With great power, comes great responsibility.

Stan Lee

And when we think we lead,

we are most led.

Lord Byron